ArtScroll® Youth Series

Rabbi Nosson Scherman / Rabbi Gedaliah Zlotowitz
General Editors
Rabbi Meir Zlotowitz ז"ל, *Founder*

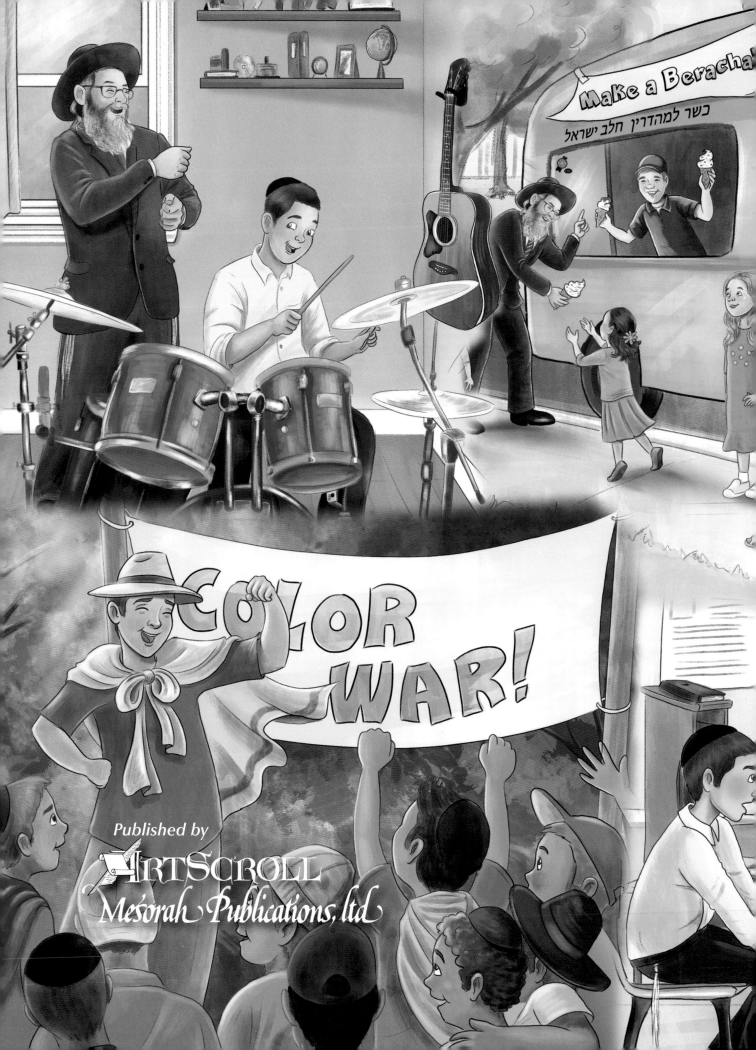

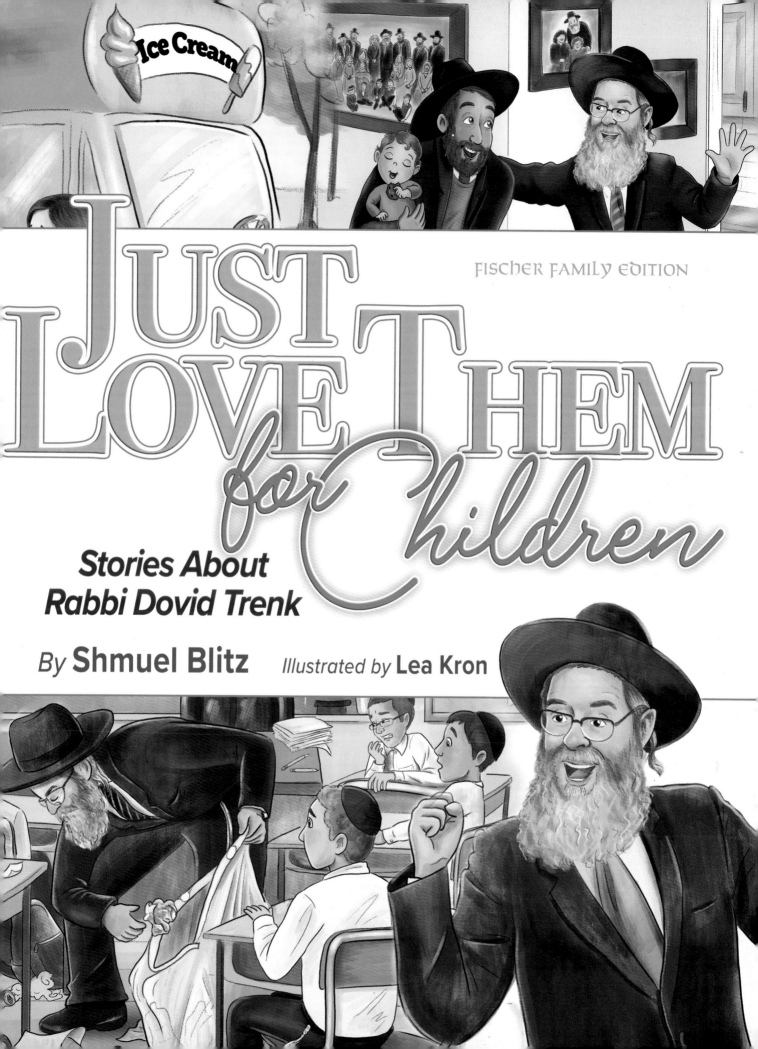

FISCHER FAMILY EDITION

JUST LOVE THEM for Children

Stories About Rabbi Dovid Trenk

By **Shmuel Blitz**   Illustrated by **Lea Kron**

We are proud to dedicate this book in honor of

Our Children נ״י

It is also dedicated in honor of

my friends and
my extended Adelphia family.

We were fortunate to be a part of a wonderful, sincere,
and devoted group of talmidim who consider Adelphia
our second home, with Rebbeim like Rabbi Trenk and
Rabbi Shain, who taught us lifelong lessons.

May our children have the z'chus to be part of such a family
and may they give us boundless Torah nachas in good health.

Shloimie and Chaya Fischer

FISCHER ROOFING

The author dedicates this book to his grandson
Lior Blitz

First Impression: July 2021
ARTSCROLL® SERIES "JUST LOVE THEM FOR CHILDREN"
© *Copyright 2021 by* Mesorah Publications, Ltd., 313 Regina Avenue / Rahway, NJ 07065 / (718) 921-9000 / www.artscroll.com

ISBN-10: 1-4226-2849-3 / ISBN-13: 978-1-4226-2849-2
Printed in PRC

Table of Contents

The Youngest Teacher

Everyone knows that Rabbi Dovid Trenk was an amazing rebbi. But very few people know that he started teaching long before he was a grown man. It began when he was just 5 years old.

A man named Gerard Wortkin was the head of a famous museum in New York City. One day, while reading a newspaper, he saw an advertisement for the Adelphia Yeshivah. It mentioned its *menahel*, its principal, Rabbi Dovid Trenk.

"Oh my," he thought. "Dovid Trenk? I have not seen him for almost 60 years. I must call him today."

But, how did Mr. Wortkin know Rabbi Trenk?

As a young boy, Dovid Trenk grew up in Boro Park, in Brooklyn. He lived in an older building on 12th Avenue with many other families. His parents sent him to yeshivah. But many of the other Jewish boys were not as lucky. They went to public school, and often they knew very little about being Jewish.

Gerard was one of those boys. He lived in the same building as Dovid and they played together every day after school. Once, Dovid brought a gift to his friend Gerard. It was a book about the *alef-beis*.

Both Dovid and Gerard were only 5 years old. Dovid explained to his friend, "I know there are many things they do not teach you in public school. Please let me teach you about being Jewish."

Every day, both of them would sit together. Dovid taught Gerard the *alef-beis*, and a little bit about the holidays and some Chumash.

Then something terrible happened. Gerard's father passed away when Gerard was only 9 years old. Dovid visited his apartment every day to comfort both his friend and the family.

Now, almost 60 years later, Gerard met Rabbi Trenk again. At their meeting Gerard told him, "You taught me the *alef-beis*. You taught me a little bit about being Jewish. So, my old friend, you are my rebbi. You were the only

one who came to visit my family after my father passed away. I want to thank you so much for that!"

Even as a 5-year-old, Dovid's greatest joy was making sure people learned what it meant to be a Jew.

The Test

It was Thursday morning and Dovid Trenk woke up bright and early. He had been waiting for this day for a very long time.

"Let's go, let's go," his father called. "We don't want to be late. Today we are going to RJJ Yeshivah. They will give you a test to see if you are accepted there. It is a wonderful school."

Dovid dressed quickly and ate breakfast. Then he and his father walked together to the train station. Both were nervous. Would Dovid do well? Would they accept him into the yeshivah?

Soon after they arrived, the principal, Rabbi Hillel Weiss, called Dovid into his office. Both father and son walked in together. Rabbi Weiss asked Dovid the first question on Chumash. Dovid did not know the answer, so his father answered for him.

Rabbi Weiss asked a second question. Feeling a little nervous, Dovid did not know the answer again. And again, his father answered for him.

Rabbi Weiss thought for a moment, and then asked a third question. "Dovid, can you play ball?"

This time Dovid answered himself. "Yes, I can. I can play very well."

"That is wonderful," said Rav Weiss. "That is very important. You are accepted into our yeshivah."

A giant smile appeared on Dovid's face.

⊙ ⊙ ⊙

Many years later, when Rav Dovid Trenk was the *menahel* at Adelphia Yeshivah, a young man entered his office, ready to be tested to see if he would be accepted into the yeshivah.

As soon as Rav Trenk closed the door, and no one else could hear, the boy looked up and whispered, "Rabbi Trenk, I am very sorry but I cannot even read one Rashi. I do not know how to learn at all."

Rav Trenk remembered that day, so long ago, when he was young. He remembered how he was nervous and could not answer a single question

that the principal had asked. And he remembered how the principal had made him feel good, and had accepted him anyway.

A giant smile appeared on his face. "That, my friend, is exactly why you are here. To learn. Welcome to Adelphia Yeshivah. Now we will teach you *how* to learn."

Rabbi Trenk never saw weakness in his students. He saw only their strengths. He saw what they could do, if they tried hard enough.

But It Is Just a Few Coins

Dovid was one of the first campers to go to Camp Munk after it opened. All through the year he looked forward to July and August, when he would be there for the summer.

Camp was a time for sports, playing with other boys, and learning. Dovid fit in well, and everyone loved him. He had a great jump shot in basketball, could play any position in baseball, and he loved to learn.

Every part of the summer was just great.

Today, things at camp are a little different than they were years ago. Now, it is easy to make phone calls and to be in touch with friends and family. Then, there were just two public phones next to each other. Erev Shabbos, the boys would line up and use these phones to call their parents and wish them a Good Shabbos.

Since the phones were right next to each other, there was no privacy. Everyone heard everything that was said.

Suddenly there was loud yelling on one of the phones. "No. You don't understand," the boy shouted. "I need you to tell me where!"

It seems that Dovid Trenk had made a phone call. Something was wrong with the phone, and when he hung up, the coins he had put into it to make the call fell down onto the floor.

He immediately dialed the telephone company. "I need to return this money to your company!" he explained. "I made a phone call, and the money came back but it belongs to you."

"It is okay. Forget about it," the woman replied. "It is just a few coins. Just keep it. The telephone company doesn't care."

Dovid insisted. "That would be stealing. I will not steal. Please tell me where I can send the money. I cannot keep this money."

She had never heard anything like this in all the years she worked for the phone company. This boy was different.

Finally, she gave Dovid the address of the phone company. Right away,

Dovid put the money in the mail. Then, he was able to start Shabbos with a big smile.

Even as a young boy, Dovid Trenk was different. The idea of stealing, even just a few coins, was something he could not accept. Not then. Not ever.

The Ice Cream Truck

I f you were once a *talmid* of Rabbi Dovid Trenk, you were always a *talmid* of his. It did not matter how far away you lived, or how much time had passed, you were always connected to him.

Yossel, who had been one of his *talmidim* many years before, sat in Rabbi Trenk's house. Yossel was crying. His wife was very ill. He davened for her, he gave *tzedakah* for her to get better, but nothing seemed to help. Every day she became weaker and weaker.

"I don't know what to do," Yossel wept to Rabbi Trenk. "Nothing I try works. Nothing the doctors do seems to help her."

Rabbi Trenk felt so sad. His heart broke. Tears streamed down his cheeks. He felt all the pain that Yossel felt.

"I have an idea," he whispered. "Let's make a *berachos* party in your wife's merit. We will bring together a large group of children and they will say *berachos* in her honor."

Other people might just have brought a few children and asked each one to say a *berachah*. But that was not how Rabbi Trenk did things.

He invited hundreds of children from the neighborhood to be at Yossel's house the next day, at 2:00 in the afternoon, for the big surprise.

Then Rabbi Trenk rented an ice cream truck. He told the driver to park it in front of Yossel's house.

"There is nothing in the world as holy as the *berachos* that children make," Rabbi Trenk told Yossel.

At 2:00, all the children in the neighborhood lined up for their ice cream. One by one they received their treat. And one by one each child recited the *berachah* in a loud voice, while everyone else answered, "Amen!"

Each child concentrated very hard on the meaning of every word. They had in mind that this mitzvah should help Yossel's wife get better.

Rabbi Trenk stayed next to the truck all afternoon, handing out ice cream. After each child said a *berachah* he, too, shouted out "Amen."

Yossel's wife listened from inside the house. She thanked Hashem for the miracle she knew would be coming.

Rabbi Dovid Trenk did things his own way. And very often Hashem helped get the results he needed!

The Crowded Supermarket

It was a busy shopping day in Lakewood, New Jersey. People were loading their carts with fruits, vegetables, breakfast cereal, ice cream, and everything else you can imagine.

Rabbi Trenk had finished shopping. Soon, it would be his turn to pay. He got ready to put his groceries onto the counter.

Suddenly, a cellphone rang. It belonged to the woman standing right in front of him in line. As she answered the phone, everyone could hear the yelling coming out of the phone. "I will not watch your boys anymore," the babysitter screamed. "Not even for another minute," her voice was clearly heard by all. "You get home right now!" she shouted. "I am walking out of your house in five minutes. Not one minute more. This place is a zoo!"

The woman's face turned bright red. She was so embarrassed! But what could she do? She needed her groceries, but she could not leave her children home without a babysitter.

Rabbi Trenk smiled warmly at her. "Do not worry, not even for one second. You go home and take care of your beautiful *kinderlach*. Leave me your address and I will deal with all your groceries."

The woman didn't know what to say. She ran out of the store, jumped into her car, and rushed home.

Back in the store, Rabbi Trenk paid for her groceries and then for his own. He carefully packed her groceries into four boxes, making sure nothing would get damaged. He loaded everything into his car and drove to the woman's house.

"Here are your groceries," he told her when she answered the doorbell. "And I have no doubt that you have the finest boys around. They will grow to become great *talmidei chachamim*. Just love them!"

Even though Rabbi Trenk had never met this person before, he jumped at the opportunity to help her. He always knew what people needed. And he even made her feel good about her children!

Eating at Adelphia Yeshivah

Growing boys need to eat. Growing boys love to eat. And Adelphia Yeshivah was filled with growing boys.

One evening a group of students were sitting together talking. "I am really hungry," one complained. "You bet. So am I," said another.

"Let's break into the kitchen and get some real food," suggested a third.

Quietly, the group walked together down to the kitchen. They were going to break the lock and see what food they could take. They knew they weren't allowed, but…

Standing right there at the kitchen door was Rabbi Trenk. "How are you doing, boys?" he asked. He understood right away what was going on. He understood that they were hungry and were planning to break into the kitchen.

They all stared at one another and then at the floor, not sure how to answer. They were all embarrassed and afraid they would be punished.

Rabbi Trenk looked at them and smiled, one of his big friendly smiles that always made people feel so good about themselves. He decided not to mention that the boys were up after bedtime. He also decided not to mention that they were planning to break into the kitchen to take food.

"C'mon guys. Let's all go to my house and get something good to eat."

All the boys followed their rebbi to his house. He took out a giant pot from the closet, filled it with water, and turned on the stove. The water began to boil. Next, he took a few packages of spaghetti, broke the long sticks in half and dropped them into the pot. Then he cut up slabs of butter and dropped that in. "This will make it especially tasty," he explained.

In another pot, he began making tomato sauce. It was like watching a chef in a fancy restaurant.

A little while later, the hungry boys received their plates filled with spaghetti and sauce. They gobbled it up. Each knew how lucky he was to have such a special rebbi.

Years later, when Rabbi Trenk met up with one of these boys he said, "Remember the spaghetti we all made that night? Wasn't it delicious?" He understood the best way to connect with these boys was not by yelling at them, but by loving them.

The Summer Job

Rabbi Trenk understood how important the summer was for his students. He realized it was a time for them to enjoy themselves. But he also knew that it was a time when they could either grow stronger in their *Yiddishkeit* or become weaker.

For this reason, he convinced many of them to come with him to Camp Munk. He wanted them to have a great time. Even more important, he wanted them to grow both in their learning and in their actions.

One of his students, Ephraim, could not go to camp. It was too expensive and his parents could not afford it.

So Rabbi Trenk worked hard to find him the right job for the summer. He knew that Ephraim needed a strict schedule to keep him busy all day. Rabbi Trenk would not stop until he found him the perfect job. And he did. There was an opening at a local Lakewood Jewish bookstore.

"Ephraim, I found you a wonderful job in a Torah environment," Rabbi Trenk told him. "You will be working in a bookstore selling Jewish books. What could be better?"

But Ephraim was not sure he wanted to be working during the summer. "I don't know, Rebbi," he replied. "I thought that I would just relax and take it easy. Then I will be more ready to start yeshivah in September."

"Trust me," Rabbi Trenk insisted. "I know you. You will love it and they will love you."

One day that summer, Rabbi Trenk walked into the store. He went right over to Ephraim and asked, "How is it going here?"

Ephraim smiled and told him, "It is really great. You were so right. I get along so well with all the customers. It is actually fun. And they are even paying me to have fun."

Ephraim didn't realize that Rabbi Trenk had driven more than three hours just to spend a few minutes with his student and make sure he was doing okay!

Who else would drive from Camp Munk in the Catskill Mountains to Lakewood, New Jersey, just to speak for ten minutes to one of his students?

A Mother Like Mine

A tall man was at a wedding, dancing in front of the *chassan*. His face was glowing. The *chassan's* face also glowed. The man was jumping and singing, and making everyone there happy.

Later, a woman approached him and said, "Rabbi Trenk, I have a special request for you. Please give me a *berachah*."

"A *berachah* from me?" he asked. "Why from me?"

"I want a very special *berachah*," she replied. "I want my son to grow up to be just like you."

Rabbi Trenk smiled kindly and answered, "To have a son like me, a person must have had a mother like mine."

Who was Rabbi Dovid Trenk's mother? Who was his father? Why were they so special?

Reb Shea Trenk, his father, arrived in America from Europe as a young man. He was able to learn in yeshivah for only two years. After that, he had to go to work to help support his family. Even so, he spent all his free time learning until he, too, was able to give *shiurim* in his shul. He became a great *talmid chacham*.

Rabbi Trenk's mother, Batsheva, or Shirley as she was called, was a very special and holy woman. After she married Reb Shea, she brought her husband's sick mother, Babba Leah, into their tiny apartment to live with them. Batsheva cared for her faithfully. The Trenks even borrowed money to buy expensive medicines for her. There was only one bedroom in their apartment, but Batsheva gave it to Babba Leah. Batsheva and her husband slept on a mattress on the floor in the dining room.

Later on, after Reb Shea's mother passed away, Batsheva brought her own mother, Babba Golda, to live with them in their apartment. She lovingly took care of her, making her as comfortable as she could.

Rabbi Trenk knew he came from very special parents. But he was modest, and did not see himself as special. He only saw the good in others.

Just Give Him a Little Time

In Camp Munk, any time a counselor had a camper who would not behave, he would turn to Rabbi Trenk for help. They would often tell him, "What do I do with this boy? He is making me crazy."

Rabbi Trenk would usually just laugh and answer, "Oh, you weren't here years ago. The things the boys did then were much worse than what they do today. Just give him a little time and a little love."

One summer, the new learning director was Rabbi Duvie Morgenstern. He approached Rabbi Trenk one afternoon and said, "There is this one boy, Chaim, who was constantly disrupting his entire group. He bothered the boys and they didn't want him around. So I decided to learn with him one-on-one, just the two of us, away from all the others. But I see that I am still getting nowhere. What should I do with him?"

"Everything will be fine," Rabbi Trenk smiled. "He is young, he is new in camp, and you have to give him a little time. Just have patience and make sure to stick with him."

Rabbi Morgenstern did just that. He followed Rabbi Trenk's advice completely.

The summer ended and the next summer began. Again, Rabbi Morgenstern worked closely with Chaim. And the next summer again.

Each year Chaim showed great improvement, becoming very popular with the other boys.

Finally, nine years later, Color War began in Camp Munk. This was the grand finale of the summer, the time that all the campers looked forward to.

Chaim was picked to be general of one of the Color War teams! He beamed with pride as he stood in front of his group of boys, leading the troops.

Rabbi Trenk walked past Rabbi Morgenstern with a giant smile on his face. He quietly pointed to Chaim and asked, "Reb Duvie, remember him?"

Nothing more needed to be said. Rabbi Morgenstern had worked hard

and had really helped this boy grow. But it was Rabbi Trenk who had helped Reb Duvie.

Even after nine years, Rabbi Trenk remembered everything about each of the boys. He was sure everyone could succeed. Even the learning directors.

Up Is Down, Back Is Front

It was the first day of summer camp, and learning group was scheduled to begin at 11:00 in the morning.

The campers in Rabbi Trenk's group made sure to arrive on time. They wanted to make a good first impression. Each one was in the Camp Munk annex at 11:00 sharp, ready to start.

11:00. Everyone sat waiting. 11:02, no Rabbi Trenk. 11:05, still no Rabbi Trenk. *Where is he?* they wondered. Finally, at ten minutes after 11, Rabbi Trenk entered. He walked around the table where the boys were sitting and smiled at each camper.

Finally, he sat down at the far back end of the table. He opened his Gemara and in his usual booming voice began, "Okay. Let's go, guys. Let's learn."

The boys were confused. Why isn't rebbi sitting at the front of the table? Why is he sitting in the back?

That evening, Shimi, one of the boys in the group, approached him and asked. "Why did Rebbi sit in the back? Rebbis always sit at the front of the table."

Rabbi Trenk chuckled and said, "All the top learners sit in the front. They are going to listen to me no matter where I sit. That is why they sit in the front, to be closer to their rebbi."

Shimi waited impatiently for Rabbi Trenk to continue.

"The other guys, the ones less interested in learning, always go to the back where they think I am not going to bother them. So, I always walk in late on the first day to first see where everyone is sitting. Then I take my place in the back with the "back of the room *chevrah.*"

Shimi burst out laughing. "You are so right, Rebbi. That is exactly why I went to the back of the table, so you wouldn't bother me and I could just relax."

"Yes!" Rabbi Trenk answered. "It is exactly boys like you that I want to be near. That I need to be near."

Nobody understood teenage boys better than Rabbi Trenk. He understood them better than they understood themselves.

Grandfather and Grandchildren

Many students from Adelphia Yeshivah stayed in constant touch with Rabbi Trenk even after they graduated. He was their rebbi while they were there. And he continued to be their rebbi for the rest of their lives.

It was 2011, and Rabbi Dovid Trenk was celebrating his 70th birthday. Some of his former *talmidim* came by to wish him a mazel tov.

Naftali, now a grown man with children of his own, walked in with his sons. "Rebbi, do you see these boys?" he told Rabbi Trenk. "They are your *eineklach* – your grandchildren. If not for you, I would not be who I am and they would not be who they are today!"

A giant smile appeared on Rabbi Trenk's face and he burst out laughing. "Usually, I would never let one of my students say such a thing. This is really just about you. But in this case I will accept your compliment."

Naftali stared at him wondering what he meant.

"Do you remember that after you left Adelphia you went to another yeshivah?" Rabbi Trenk continued. "You did not behave well there. The Rosh Yeshivah felt you would do better somewhere else. I heard about it, called the Rosh Yeshivah, and tried to change his mind. I was sure that was where you belonged."

Naftali had never heard about this. He listened carefully, anxious to hear the rest of the story.

"I tried so many ways to convince him, but nothing helped. Then I had an idea. I told him how your parents suffered in Europe during World War II. After the War, they had children, but you were the only one they were able to send to yeshivah. I suggested that maybe Hashem helped them survive through the War in order to have a son like you!"

Tears streamed down Naftali's cheeks as he listened to his rebbi speak.

"I told the Rosh Yeshivah that he cannot send you to a different yeshivah. After hearing this story, he agreed to keep you there. So yes, you are

right. These really are my *eineklach*. I am so happy to be able to share them with you."

Rabbi Trenk rarely took credit for things he did for others. This was a special case where a boy's life as a Torah Jew was saved just because of him.

The Painter

Yossi was not behaving in his yeshivah. He was very unhappy, and did not want to be there.

"What is going to be with you, Yossi?" his father asked. "You know you cannot continue acting this way. You must learn to behave yourself."

Yossi looked at his father and said, "A friend told me that I should try Adelphia Yeshivah. Maybe we can go there and I will take their entrance test."

His father smiled. "Yes. That would be wonderful."

Really, Yossi thought this would just be a giant waste of time. He didn't think that there was any place where he could succeed. But he wanted so much to please his father.

The next day the two of them drove to New Jersey to meet with the *menahel* of Adelphia Yeshivah.

They parked their car in the lot by the school, got out, and walked toward the yeshivah building.

A tall man, wearing painter's clothing and a painter's cap, was up on a ladder working. He noticed them and called out, "Wait one minute. I will be right down. I am up here getting the yeshivah ready for opening day next week."

Father and son looked at him. They wondered who this was. They were both confused.

The man climbed down the ladder and introduced himself. "Welcome to Adelphia Yeshivah. I am Rabbi Dovid Trenk. And I assume you are Yossi," he said to the boy.

Yossi just stared at him, wide-eyed. This was not what he expected. He had never seen anything like this before. *A menahel dressed like this and painting a building?*

Rabbi Trenk whispered to Yossi. "I hope you know a little bit about

painting buildings. I need all the help I can get. And afterward we can sit down and learn a little. I need people just like you in this yeshivah."

Yossi's father drove home. Now he was the one with a smile on his face. He knew that his son had finally found the best place for him – and the best possible rebbi also.

Rabbi Trenk never just looked at a person. He was able to look inside a person. He knew there was so much good inside everyone.

Clean Up

One morning, Rabbi Trenk walked into his classroom and saw a big mess. Papers were piled up all over the floor, the garbage pail was lying upside down, and two desks were turned on their side.

Feeling a bit frustrated, he stared at the boys and said, "This is no way to learn Torah. This classroom is a mess. It is not proper *kavod* for the Torah to have a classroom look like this."

He walked around the room, looking at each boy. "I will tell you what," he smiled. "I am going to walk out of the room for five full minutes. When I return I want you to have this room spotless and clean."

He walked out into the hall. The students got up and slowly began going through the motions of cleaning up. A tissue here, a few papers there. One person even picked up one of the desks and turned it right side up.

After five minutes, Rabbi Trenk returned and looked around the classroom. The classroom was still a mess.

Instead of yelling at them, he walked around the room, bent over, and started picking up the garbage from the floor.

With their faces red from embarrassment, a few of the boys jumped up, wanting to help him.

"We are sorry, Rebbi," each one said. "We should have done more to clean up this room. You are right. We needed to make it a place where one can learn Torah properly. We will take care of it."

Rabbi Trenk picked up his hand and said, "I am sorry, boys. You lost your chance. Now, stay in your seats."

"But, we want to help," one cried.

"Sorry, but the answer is no," he replied. "Now it is my mitzvah to clean the room. Maybe next time you will have the chance for it to become your mitzvah, but not this time."

He continued bent over, picking up all the pieces of trash and putting them in the garbage bag.

Rabbi Trenk knew the best way for students to truly learn was by example. Watching their rebbi bent down toward the floor, doing what they should have done, was a lesson they would never forget.

What a Question!

Nachum was not doing well in his yeshivah.

His father had been Rabbi Trenk's student in Yeshivah High School, and now had an idea.

"I have great news for you, Nachum," his father said. "I just spoke to my rebbi from high school, Rabbi Dovid Trenk, and he invited you to stay at his house for Shabbos. He is so much fun. You will have a great time!"

"Sorry, Abba," Nachum answered. "I am not really interested."

"Just one Shabbos," his father said. "If I am wrong, you will just come home Sunday and tell me that you were right and I was wrong."

That Shabbos, Nachum went to the Trenks. He had a great time. The Rabbi, the Rebbetzin, and all their kids were wonderful. He laughed and had fun the entire Shabbos.

Sunday morning came. Nachum was packing his bag and getting ready to go home. Rebbetzin Leah Trenk walked into his room, and said, "Nachum, it was so great having you for Shabbos. We all want you to come back again soon. But, while you are here anyway, why don't you go visit Rabbi Trenk in his classroom where he is now teaching?"

With nothing better to do, Nachum walked over to Adelphia Yeshivah and sat down in Rabbi Trenk's classroom.

He was teaching Chumash. After sitting for over an hour, Nachum raised his hand and asked a question.

Rabbi Trenk's eyes opened wide, and for a few seconds he stood as still as a statue. Then, he began to jump up and down. "Nachum, I must tell you. I have been teaching this *parashah* every year for many years. In all this time, nobody, and I mean nobody, has ever asked this question!"

Rabbi Trenk became very excited. "We must call your father right now and repeat this question to him!"

This is the first time a rebbi ever wanted to call my father to tell him something nice about me, Nachum thought. *It has always been about something bad.*

Nachum did not go home that day. Instead, he stayed in Adelphia Yeshivah and went on to learn much Torah there.

Rabbi Trenk always knew what each student needed. And how best to give it to him.

The Bellyache

An 11-year-old boy was walking down the path in Camp Munk. He was bent over, his right hand covering his stomach.

"Ow, ow, ow," he moaned.

Suddenly, a very tall man appeared right in front of him. "What is the matter?" he asked. "It looks like you are in pain."

Tears formed in the boy's eyes. "Yes," he cried, "my belly hurts so much. I went to the nurse this morning, but she told me I was fine and there was nothing wrong with me. But it hurts!"

"I am so sorry to hear that," the man answered. "First, let me introduce myself. My name is Rabbi Dovid Trenk. Now, tell me your name."

"My name is Chaim," he answered.

"Chaim. A very nice name. And tell me your parents' names, please," Rabbi Trenk continued.

The boy answered and Rabbi Trenk became very excited. "Yes, yes, yes. I know your *zeidy* well. He is my good friend. One thing I know about him is that he loves to run. Sometimes, he even runs in long marathons."

Rabbi Trenk suddenly began to run. He grabbed Chaim by the elbow and the two began to run together. People watched them and began laughing. It was very funny to see this tall bearded rabbi running down the path holding onto his hat with one hand and this young boy's elbow with the other.

The boy also started to laugh. A big smile appeared on his face. They ran together all the way down the path.

Finally, they stopped. Rabbi Trenk suddenly became serious. "Let me explain something to you. You are smiling and laughing now. But just a few minutes ago, you were crying and in pain. This is how life is. Sometimes you will be happy and sometimes you will be sad. But all you need to do is laugh and smile and the pain will usually go away. That is a very important secret for you to learn."

Little Chaim remembered this advice all his life. Right then he decided that this was how he would be. Smiling and laughing.

The Bar Mitzvah Boy

Ephraim's big day was finally here. It was the day of his Bar Mitzvah. Party. Relatives. Friends. Presents. All coming today to celebrate his special day.

One by one everyone began entering the hall. Tante Helen, Uncle Harold, Grandpa Abe, Grandma Bella. Everyone was there.

Then his rebbi stood up to speak. "My sweet little Ephraim. I hope that one day you are going to be a very good boy." Ephraim noticed that he didn't say how good he was, but how good he could become.

Next, his father spoke. "Ephraim is my *bechor*, my oldest son. I hope that one day he is going to make me very proud of him."

I guess he is not proud of me today," Ephraim thought.

You see, Ephraim was a very mischievous child. He often got into trouble in school. Wherever the fun was, that is where he could be found. At home, Ephraim often teased his younger brother. He thought it was fun, but his little brother certainly did not!

Ephraim had heard enough. In the middle of the next speech, he went outside to the lobby to play with his friends. "Nobody had even one nice thing to say about me," he told his good friend, Shlomo. "Only that maybe one day I might become good."

Rabbi Trenk, a neighbor, was attending this Bar Mitzvah and was sitting in the back of the hall. He saw everything that was happening. He, too, slipped out of the hall and went over to Ephraim. "Mazel tov, mazel tov, Ephraim." With a big smile he took Ephraim's hand and shook it until a grin finally appeared on Ephraim's face.

"My Ephraim'l," he began. "I wish I could have made a speech about you. I know who you really are. I know how much you love life. I know how you make everyone smile and laugh. I know how special you are. I wish it had been me speaking about you. I know what a special boy you are right now. It is a pity that everyone else does not see that yet."

Rabbi Trenk was very sensitive and always knew when a child was upset.
He knew exactly what needed to be said to make someone feel better.

The Change

School did not interest Gershon at all.

He would sit in the back of the classroom and lay his head down on the desk during class. It made no difference who the rebbi was. He just counted the days until he would not have to go to school anymore.

Even at home, he did not talk much to his family. He stayed in his room listening to music or reading a magazine.

"Gershon, please come down now for supper," his mother called. Slowly Gershon picked himself up out of bed and walked down the stairs. He walked into the kitchen, quietly sat down in his chair and ate supper.

Not a word to any of his brothers. Not a word to his sister. And hardly a word to either of his parents.

One by one, each would try to talk to him, but he would answer just by nodding his head or grunting.

This made the entire family very sad.

Then, one day, in eighth grade, toward the end of the year, Gershon sat up at his desk in class. He started listening to what the rebbi was saying.

He came home and began talking to his family.

Over that summer, the boy's mother called Rabbi Trenk, a friend of the family, to share the good news.

"Rabbi Trenk, I just don't understand it. He talks with us, and he began paying attention in yeshivah. Now, over the summer he even arranged a *chavrusa* to learn with in order to get ready for next year."

Later that day, Rabbi Trenk called Gershon's rebbi. "Did you hear the great news about Gershon?"

"Yes, I did," the rebbi answered. "It is truly amazing. A miracle."

"I have a question for you," Rabbi Trenk added. "Do you think the boy changed?"

"Yes, I do. It is an amazing change," he answered.

"No, no, no. That is not what happened," Rabbi Trenk said. "He did not

change. This is exactly who he was all along. The only thing that changed is that now we can see who Gershon really is."

Every boy was perfect in Rabbi Trenk's eyes. Sometimes it just took longer to actually see. Sometimes someone had to help the child along, and sometimes it just happened by itself. Just make sure to always be there for him.

The Bowling Alley

Hillel and Chaya Sarah Jaffa were spending a pleasant vacation at the Dead Sea in Eretz Yisrael. The sun was shining and the water was shimmering.

One evening they went for a stroll. They walked into a store to buy gifts for their children back home in America.

"Look how cute these things are," Chaya Sarah said to her husband. "I am sorry that our vacation is ending, but I am really looking forward to seeing our kids again and giving them these presents."

A man standing in the aisle heard them speaking to each other. "Hi there. How are you?" he said in perfect English. "Are you having a good time here at the Dead Sea?"

"It is so beautiful," Hillel replied. "I see you are from America also. Where are you from?"

"Freehold, New Jersey," the man replied. "Did you ever hear of it?"

"Hear of it?" Hillel grinned. "I went to yeshivah right next door to Freehold."

"Don't tell me you went to Adelphia Yeshivah," the man said. "My name is Lenny. Maybe you remember me. I owned the bowling alley right near the yeshivah. The boys would often come Saturday night with their rabbi and go bowling."

"Of course I do," Hillel said. "I was one of those boys. We went with our rabbi, Rabbi Dovid Trenk."

Lenny's voice became soft, remembering those days. "Those were wonderful times. And you were such nice boys. But what I remember most is your rabbi. I never saw a teacher like him. He would drive you boys to the bowling alley and sit there, just watching everyone have fun. What I remember most was the giant angelic smile on his face. You could see how much he loved each one of you. It was so nice for me to watch."

Lenny and Hillel shook hands, said good night, both remembering the

very special warmth of Rabbi Dovid Trenk.

Rabbi Dovid Trenk was a person that people remembered and spoke about. He left his mark on so many people. Everywhere in the world.

Milk and Cookies

Rabbi Trenk loved to swim early in the morning before everyone woke up. He also loved playing baseball and basketball with the boys.

Everyone understood that learning was the most important thing, but sports were also important. Sports helped the boys stay healthy and happy. Rabbi Trenk often umpired during baseball games or coached a basketball team. Sometimes, he even shot hoops on the basketball court with the campers.

In Camp Munk, between the second and third activity period, everyone would receive a snack of milk and cookies. It was fun and really delicious.

In his jolly and booming voice, Rabbi Trenk would announce over the loudspeaker system, "Time for milk and cookies." Then he would start to sing, "Everybody, it is time for milk and cookies. Come right now."

One day he realized, *I have been doing this all wrong. I should not be saying it is time for milk and cookies, since we say the berachah of mezonos on cookies before we say the berachah of shehakol on milk. I should be saying that it is time for cookies and milk. Then it will be in the correct order.*

From that day on, every afternoon, Rabbi Trenk could be heard singing into the microphone, "Cookies and milk. It is time for cookies and milk. Remember, *mezonos* before *shehakol*. Cookies and milk. *Mezonos* before *shehakol.*"

All the campers loved this. Now they had a delicious snack together with a learning lesson at the same time! It also taught them that everything they did in life was in some way connected to halachah.

Rabbi Dovid Trenk made sure everyone's life was balanced. Whether it meant balancing their learning with their playtime, or their learning with their snack time, everything had to be both fun and educational. And all for Hashem.

The Freezer

One winter afternoon, Rebbetzin Leah Trenk went to a woman's home to drop off a package. Walking into the apartment, she could not believe what she saw. The woman was so poor! There were holes in the walls, and hardly any furniture.

When the Rebbetzin's husband, Rabbi Dovid Trenk, came home that evening, she told him about what she had seen in the woman's house. "She even had her food sitting outside in the snow on the windowsill to keep it frozen, because there was no freezer inside the house. It was so sad," Rebbetzin Leah said.

Rabbi Trenk nodded his head sympathetically, but did not say a word.

The next week, without even telling his wife, he went to an appliance store and bought a brand new freezer. He used his own money to pay for it. Then he went back to Adelphia Yeshivah and picked up a few students in his car.

"Boys," he said. "Please come with me to do a big mitzvah. Help me deliver this freezer to a woman's home. This will make her very happy."

He had already told the woman that the freezer would not cost her a penny. He didn't want her to feel embarrassed, so he explained that a family had moved away and could not take it with them. "I will bring it to your home with the help of a few of my students," he explained.

For Rabbi Trenk this was just another day, and just another good deed. It was not important that anyone else knew what he'd done, not his students and not even his wife.

Rebbetzin Trenk would never have known about this, but when she was sitting *shivah* after Rabbi Trenk passed away, this woman came to visit. She told the Rebbetzin about the freezer Rabbi Trenk had brought to her and how grateful she was. The Rebbetzin quickly figured out what had really happened. No one had moved away, and her husband had gone to the store himself to buy it for her. That was who he was.

Rabbi Trenk preferred that nobody knew when he helped others. How many good deeds like this did he do during his life? Only Hashem knows!

Drums

Any time one of his boys would show any kind of talent, Rabbi Trenk would see it as the most wonderful thing in the world.

Eli, a student in Adelphia Yeshivah, taught himself how to play keyboard. Rabbi Trenk treated him like a "real" musician, not just a beginner.

He would bring Eli along to people's houses to do *chesed*. Eli would play, the rebbi would schmooze, and everyone would be smiling. One day, they went together to visit a young boy in Williamsburg who was not well. They did not even know him. They just came to play for him and make him happy.

With Rabbi Trenk urging him on, Eli also taught himself how to play the drums. One day, while he was practicing, Eli saw his rebbi standing right behind him with imaginary drumsticks and an imaginary drum, playing right along.

Eli grew up to become a successful adult, who helped many people in his neighborhood.

The years passed quickly. "Maybe it is time for me to start learning Daf Yomi," Eli thought. And he did! Seven-and-a-half years later, he was ready to make a *siyum* on all of Shas. There was only one place he wanted to make his *siyum* — at the Adelphia Yeshivah yearly dinner.

Eli stood at the head table, looking around the room at all the people. He began to say the Hadran, the blessing said when a person makes a *siyum*.

Suddenly, he felt someone standing right behind him. It was his rebbi, Rabbi Trenk, looking over Eli's shoulder into his Gemara.

"Wow," Eli thought. "Everything in my life is connected. Rabbi Trenk was behind me when I learned to play drums. Now he's behind me when I've finished Shas! Now and then, Rabbi Trenk was always there, cheering me on. Pushing me forward."

For Rabbi Dovid Trenk, everyone was an expert. And even if the person wasn't so great yet, he knew that one day he would be.